CHURCH ANNOUNCEMENTS

J. Anthony Brown

KKT Publishing Company   Los Angeles

Upcoming Books by J. Anthony Brown

Player's Rules
Sing to the Tune
What's On Your Mind

IF THE FOLLOWING PEOPLE HAD READ THIS BOOK,
THIS IS PROBABLY WHAT THEY WOULD HAVE SAID:

Puff Daddy:
"I couldn't put it down. I can't wait to sample some of
the announcements on my next CD."

O.J. Simpson:
"Where are the pictures of the white women?"

The Chihuahua:
"Yo quiero Reverend Adenoids!"

Kirk Franklin & God's Property:
KF: "GP, are you wit me?"
GP: "Oh, yeah, it's some funny stuff in there!"

For sales information, contact:
KKT Publishing Company
1304 N. Highland Avenue, Suite 282
Hollywood, CA 90028
(877) 574-4780

ISBN 0-9675935-1-4
Contributions from Jerome Miller
Cover design by David McAdoo
Design layout by Black Butterfly Consulting

Printed in Hong Kong
10 9 8 7 6 5 4 3 2

ACKNOWLEDGEMENTS

I want to thank the following for all of their contributions:

TOM JOYNER for allowing me to do the character.

YOLANDA STARKS for getting me the job on the TJMS.

MYRA J. AND MS. DUPRE who are my road dogs and fellow comedians--two good dudes.

SYBIL WILKES who was the inspiration for Reverend Adenoids.

GEORGE WALLACE and his mama and whoever his real daddy is.

KAY PATTERSON who is my all-time favorite teacher, my favorite senator, and the one person who introduced me to books other than those that have centerfolds.

MY SISTER who has a husband and 13 kids; she is very religious and thinks I should never have written this book.

MORE ACKNOWLEDGEMENTS

MARY FLOWERS BOYCE who is a Quiet Genius (Q.G.).*

SEAN JENNINGS AKA SEAN E. MAC: "Keep doing your best."

KATHY WESTFIELD for typing up everything and for being my very special partner in crime--"Sister Black."

JEROME MILLER for helping me out with Church Announcements when I was in a pinch.

TERRY ADKINS for remembering where I'm supposed to go to. He is an accomplished artist who is probably spending too much time with me.

MELANIE ROBINSON because without her hard work and dedication, Church Announcements would never have been published. She's very blunt and to the point, but that's what I needed to get this book done.

*Her father is the real genius.

Contents

Church Announcements

REV. ADENOIDS

CHURCH ANNOUNCEMENTS

Th___ ___r has decided
___x the squeaky
___ at the back of the
___rch. Says that's
___ way he can tell
___ members are
___ in late.
If you've been hum___
shouter in th___

Publisher's Note

Foreword

You are about to enter the irreverent world of Reverend Richard Adenoids, III. His brash, tongue-in-cheek observations will have you laughing from the first page to the last. Reverend Adenoids is not poking fun at religion, so please don't take offense. He is merely reporting the events in his church that could, or could not happen in yours. Reverend Adenoids says the kinds of things that some of us have thought all along, but wouldn't dare say out loud. If you have never heard the Reverend on the Tom Joyner Morning Show, let me tell you—he is no hypocrite. He is not beyond exposing his own weaknesses in front of the whole congregation. Reverend Adenoids receives his inspiration from the one and only J. Anthony

Foreword

Brown. For those of you unfamiliar with Mr. Brown, let me assure you, he is the funniest man you've never heard of—yet. While reading this book, some of the Reverend's announcements will make your cheeks get tight and your stomach hurt from laughing out loud. You'll wish that the Reverend gave the announcements in your church every week. Don't take my word for it. Start reading and see for yourself.

-Tavis Smiley
Host of BET Tonight
Tom Joyner Morning Show Commentator

Dedications

To my mom and dad who never stopped believing in me.
To my kids Kisha, Takenya, and Tirrell whom I love very much.

Baptismal Notes

Next Sunday's baptisms will be conducted
the old-fashioned way--down at the river.
When Sister Arie Lee Beeberry got baptized last week,
her Jheri Curl went under and we couldn't get that moisturizer
ring out of the baptismal pool.

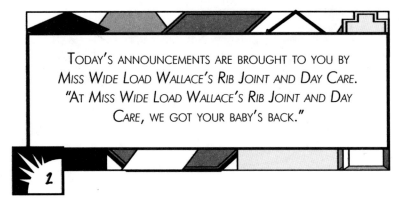

TODAY'S ANNOUNCEMENTS ARE BROUGHT TO YOU BY
MISS WIDE LOAD WALLACE'S RIB JOINT AND DAY CARE.
"AT *MISS WIDE LOAD WALLACE'S RIB JOINT AND DAY
CARE,* WE GOT YOUR BABY'S BACK."

2

Due to the high cost of water, we can no longer bring the baptismal pool up to full. So during the baptism, Miss Wide Load Wallace will sit in the tub, bring it up to full, and we'll continue the baptism.

3

IF YOU ATTENDED
THE PASTOR'S POOL PARTY
LAST SUNDAY,
IT COUNTS AS A BAPTISM.

4

Choir Rehearsals

The All Gold Tooth Choir* will rehearse right after the service. Please bring your sunglasses.

The All Male Wooden Leg Choir will have a brief meeting before the service. And remember, when returning to your seats, walk lightly.

The *All Male Toupee Choir* has requested that the ceiling fans be turned off during their number--or at least not turned on high.

6

*Choir members with toes that look like Brazil nuts are asked not to wear sandals.

Auditions for the
Men Who Act Real Feminine Choir
will be held in Meeting Room 9.
See Bishop Juan right after the service.

The Beefy Kids Choir will rehearse right after the buffet.

The Kids With Fat Fingers Choir will rehearse
in Meeting Room 3.

TODAY'S ANNOUNCEMENTS ARE BROUGHT TO YOU BY
MISS ORTHERA JOHNSON, AUTHOR OF THE BOOK,
TEN WAYS TO COVER A BIG FOREHEAD.

8

Church Fundraisers

Be sure to stop by the church store and pick up the new holy water wet wipes.

Stop by the church store to pick up the new religious communion Pez dispensers. Pull back on the head of the reverend and get saved.

So as not to be caught
short like we were last year,
the church store has stocked up on
Miss Wide Load Wallace Halloween masks.

11

TODAY'S ANNOUNCEMENTS ARE BEING SPONSORED BY
RANDY'S RENT-TO-OWN FOR THE REALLY BROKE:
"COME IN AND RENT BICYCLES, BIG WHEELS®,
BARBIE® DOLLS, BOBBY PINS, BEDROOM SLIPPERS,
STRAIGHTENING COMBS, ROTWEILERS, GOLDFISH OR
ANYTHING ELSE YOU NEED AROUND THE HOUSE."

12

Committee Meetings

"Men who wear afros that have parts on the side..."

Day	Committee Meeting	Time/Location
Daily	Men Whose Bellies Show When They Shout	At the beer truck located in back of the church around noon
Sunday	People Who Lie About Their Tithing	Auditorium during the offering
Sunday	Annual Meeting of Women Who Used to Be Fine Back in the Day and Think They Still Are	They will sashay through the aisles during the choir selection

Day	Committee Meeting	Time/Location
Sunday	Combined meeting of Kids Who Don't Know Their Daddies, Kids That Have Never Seen Their Daddies and Kids Whose Daddies Never Call Them	On Father's Day at the Pool Hall
Sunday	Women Who Like to Talk About the Pastor's Wife Behind Her Back	Ladies' Restroom after the 11:00 a.m. service
Sunday	Women Who Smell Like Liniment	Nurses' Office before the 8:00 a.m. service

Day	Committee Meeting	Time/Location
Sunday	Women Whose Dresses Ride Up in the Back	Back of the church before the 8:00 a.m. service
Sunday	Members Who Come to Church "Tore Up"	Sanctuary after the 8:00 a.m. service
Sunday	People Who Wear Shoes That Don't Match a Damn Thing	Church Office before the 5:00 p.m. service
Sunday	Small Fat Kids Who Talk Real Proper	Youth Center after church school

Day	Committee Meeting	Time/Location
Sunday	Men Who Wear White Suits and Purple Shoes	Lobby after the Easter service
Monday	Women With Less Hair on Their Heads Than Under Their Arms	Church Annex at 7:00 p.m.
Tuesday	Women Who Look Like They Smell Something	Pastor's Study after the soaps/stories
Tuesday	Women Who Look Like Paul Winfield	Usher's Lounge after the usher recruitment meeting

Day	Committee Meeting	Time/Location
Tuesday	The Two White Women To Whom No One Ever Speaks	Room 3 at 7:00 a.m.
Wednesday	Men Who Need Brassieres	Parking Lot before the field trip to Maemae's Secrets
Wednesday	Women Whose Dresses Stick to Their Butts Guest speaker: Miss Wide Load Wallace	Harvey's Piece of Meat at 12:00 p.m.

Day	Committee Meeting	Time/Location
Wednesday	Men Who Smell Like Pee	Corner of 54th and 4th after new membership class
Thursday	Big Girls Who Walk Around with a Slim Fast® shake. Please see Bishop Juan	Rooms 2 & 3
Friday	Men Who Wear Afros That Have Parts on the Sides	Church Annex before the Good Times marathon

Day	Committee Meeting	Time/Location
Saturday	Fat Kids Whose Parents Think They're Talented	Cafeteria after the Saturday morning cartoons
Saturday	Annual Meeting of Women Whose Elbows Look Like Sweet Potatoes	Miss Wide Load Wallace's house on the 25th at 1:00 p.m.
TBD	The new support group for People Who Have Low Self Esteem	Basement whenever we tell them to

Communion Notes

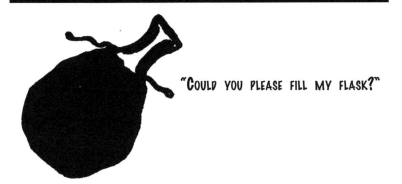

"Could you please fill my flask?"

When standing in line for communion,
please do not use the phrase,
"Could you fill my flask?"

Since it's so hot,
communion will
now be served in
wine flavored
snow cones.

TODAY'S CHURCH
ANNOUNCEMENTS ARE BROUGHT
TO YOU BY THE PEOPLE WHO
BROUGHT THEM TO YOU
LAST WEEK.
WE CAN'T CALL OUT THEIR NAMES
'CAUSE THEIR CHECK BOUNCED.

The church is
seeking volunteers
to taste test
hickory smoke,
sour cream & onion
and BBQ flavored
communion wafers.

23

To me,
the greatest
invention is the
church shot glass
for communion.
Until it came into
being, everybody
had to take a swig
and pass the bottle.

TODAY'S ANNOUNCEMENTS ARE
BROUGHT TO YOU BY
*JANICOLE'S GARDEN HOSE
BOTTLED WATER.*
"BRINGING IT OUT THE
GARDEN HOSE, 'CAUSE IT'S
CHEAPER THAT WAY."

Deacons' Corner

After a night of poker with the deacons, "Jimmy One Leg" will be known as just "Jimmy."

TODAY'S CHURCH ANNOUNCEMENTS ARE BROUGHT TO YOU BY *ARNEZ'S BED & MAKE YOUR OWN DAMN BREAKFAST*.

26

If you can't make it to church next Sunday, contact Deacon Mobley. He will stop by and pick up your church donations.

The pastor would like Deacon Rice to stop thumping the members on the head as they are praying. It's hard to concentrate when you've been thumped on the head.

The halfway house for back-sliding deacons should be open in two weeks.

27

The confessional
booth will not be in use for
the next three weeks.
Deacon Ray Jenkins will be using
it to smoke his meat.

28

Due to the recent scuffle that broke out over the weekend, Deacon Polk would like the name of the *Hide-A-Way Hotel* to be changed.

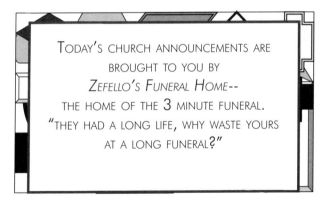

TODAY'S CHURCH ANNOUNCEMENTS ARE
BROUGHT TO YOU BY
ZEFELLO'S FUNERAL HOME--
THE HOME OF THE 3 MINUTE FUNERAL.
"THEY HAD A LONG LIFE, WHY WASTE YOURS
AT A LONG FUNERAL?"

29

Some of you complained because you couldn't understand Deacon Hartfield during this morning's prayer. He actually spoke more clearly than he usually does. He finally got his upper plate off layaway from the dentist.

TODAY'S CHURCH ANNOUNCEMENTS ARE
BROUGHT TO YOU BY
GOING THAT WAY CAB SERVICE;
"THE REASON WE CAN SAVE YOU MONEY IS
BECAUSE WE ONLY PICK YOU UP
IF WE'RE GOING THAT WAY."

30

General Announcements

Yellow Cake
(Box)

Macaroni
& Cheese
(Box)

Chicken (Fried)

Potato salad
(Too much)
Green beans
(Can)

The Standard Church Dinner

...e warden at the county jail has requested that the senior choir never come back again. Says the men have suffered enough.

TODAY'S ANNOUNCEMENTS ARE BROUGHT TO YOU BY *HATTIE MAE'S 20-MINUTE DAY CARE SERVICE*-- CALLED THAT 'CAUSE NOBODY CAN STAND YOUR KIDS LONGER THAN 20 MINUTES.

The pastor has decided to close the prayer line during the weekend--shoot, if you`ve gone this long, two more days ain`t gonna hurt you.

This goes out to whom it may concern. The pastor says, "We know you don't read the Bible at work so don't read the funny pages at church...especially while standing in line for the communion".

The pastor has decided not to fix the squeaky door at the back of the church--says that's the only way he can tell when the members are coming in late.

If you've been hurt by a shouter during the last few Sundays, the church is now offering shouters' insurance.

33

Last week's Church Theft Amnesty Day was a success. Returned were six choir robes, three collection plates, a Deacon, a speaker system...

34

Also, another reminder to all shouters. Faint time has been decreased to one minute. One minute for faint time.

All church members over 200 lbs. are being asked to bring their own spotters. If you weigh over 200 lbs. and you shout, bring your own spotters.

Due to construction, 1st Baptist Church will hold service at 2nd AME on the 3rd Sunday at 4 o'clock on 6th Street. There's no way in hell they're gonna have a crowd.

35

Starting next Sunday, anybody who rides in the church van will be asked to chip in on the gas.

TODAY'S SERVICE IS BROUGHT TO YOU BY *LENNY'S BBQ PIT AND LIQUOR STORE*: "WE'VE GOT YOUR SAUCE."

Large members are asked not to sit on the end of the church benches--makes other members feel like they're on a seesaw.

Since we introduced cognac confessions, confessions have gone up *75%*--get three or four shots in you and you get to talking.

In order to save money on weddings, the pastor has decided to re-use the rice.

TODAY'S ANNOUNCEMENTS ARE BROUGHT TO YOU BY *JIMMY JEEK'S JUKE JOINT AND TEETH CLEANING.* OUR MOTTO IS "YOU ALWAYS LEAVE WITH A NICE SMILE."

All church members, take note:
If you'd like to see the pastor's new shredder,
look in his office right under the suggestion box.

The next announcement comes from the
church accounting department:
Our prayers go out to anyone who has had
his/her taxes done by us.

After the gospel
convention in
Birmingham last week the
mayor had to declare
a state of emergency.
The city was completely out of
chicken, sweet potato pie,
greens, Kool-Aid® and
Stacey Adams®.

39

OUR SPONSOR TODAY IS
JIMMY'S TROUBLE SHOOTING COMPANY.
IF YOU'RE HAVING TROUBLE, CALL JIMMY.
HE'LL COME OUT AND SHOOT 'EM.

People who park their raggedy cars next to the
pastor's new Mercedes will be towed away.
Don't say we didn't warn you.

We're all the same in the eyes of the Man above—
but not our cars.

Starting next week, the twenty-four hour prayer request line will start taking delivery orders for chicken wings. Buy a twelve-piece bucket at the regular price and get a free prayer cloth.

For those of you with home computers, you can now see our services on-line at www.why_didn`t_you_get_your_lazy_butt_up.com. Our secured server accepts donations from Visa and Mastercard.

41

Especially for Brothers

The pastor has given the okay for jogging suits to be worn in church--you wear 'em everywhere else, why not wear 'em in church?

42

Especially for Sisters

This goes out to all of the church mothers. The word knee-high means *knee-high.*

Young mothers whose babies keep hollering during the service will be given a complimentary tape so they can hear what it sounds like when they get home.

43

Especially for Young People

Due to cutbacks, the church could only afford one Boy Scout uniform, so it will be worn on a rotation system. When you wear it, wash it and bring it back.

This message goes out to the kids who were playing with the hula hoop after the service. Please bring it back-- that was Miss Wide Load Wallace's pinkie ring.

44

We'd like to remind our Sunday School attendees that they don't get recess. That goes for senior citizens too.

45

In response to all the
complaints we got last year,
at this year's Easter egg hunt,
the kids will look for
"African-American" eggs
instead of "colored" eggs.

46

...and then there's Miss Wide Load Wallace

We apologize to all who had to take that three-mile detour this morning while Miss Wide Load Wallace was crossing the street.

We'd also like to apologize for the Mayflower® truck that was parked in the parking lot. Using it was the only way we could get Miss Wide Load Wallace to church this morning.

47

The church revival tent will be a little larger this year.
Instead of the regular tent we erected a pair of
Miss Wide Load Wallace's bloomers.

TODAY'S CHURCH ANNOUNCEMENTS ARE
BROUGHT TO YOU BY
PINKERTON WILLARD'S MANUFACTURERS,
THE PEOPLE WHO BROUGHT YOU
"CLOTHES THAT SMELL LIKE MEAT."

If you noticed that the roof is off the annex building, don`t think it's being repaired--just making room for Miss Wide Load Wallace.

Miss Wide Load Wallace was late today-- seems it took a little longer to braid her hair than she first realized.
Not on her head, on her chest.

49

We'd like to apologize for the flood in the basement during the all-you-can-eat buffet. Couldn't get Miss Wide Load Wallace to stop drooling.

Miss Wide Load Wallace will be
leaving church early next Sunday.
Church members are not to be alarmed.
The sun is not going down.

50

This weekend the Competition of the World's Strongest Man was held. Mr. Wilburt Gut won when after three hours and fifteen minutes he successfully pulled Miss Wide Load Wallace away from a plate of chicken.

51

Congratulations go out to Tanya Roberts. She is this year's winner of the "Make a Mud Pie That Looks Like Miss Wide Load Wallace" contest. She used 6 tons of mud--bless her heart--just on the hips.

Ground breaking ceremonies were held yesterday... I'm sorry, that's not correct. That was yesterday, the ground broke when Miss Wide Load Wallace fell down.

52

"Men Who Grow Hair in Their Ears"
have decided to change the name of their group
because they just signed their first female member.
Our congratulations to Miss Wide Load Wallace!

TODAY'S CHURCH ANNOUNCEMENTS
ARE BROUGHT TO YOU BY
SECOND CHANCE BEAUTY SHOP.
"IF WE MESS YOUR HAIR UP ONE TIME,
GIVE US A SECOND CHANCE."

53

Also our prayers go out to Miss Wide Load Wallace who is trying out for the Dallas Cowboys. She's trying out for the position of the little thing that the football players push-- whatever it's called.

Let's hope she makes it.

I think she has a good chance.

54

Also, over the weekend Miss Wide Load Wallace made medical history—her body rejected 40 cans of Slim Fast®.

Our congrats go out to Miss Wide Load Wallace for losing 30 pounds over the weekend. She lost her lunch.

Brother and Sister Cummings just returned from their honeymoon on Catalina Island off the coast of California. Never seen Catalina? Well, it's smaller, but almost the same size as Miss Wide Load Wallace.

For her birthday, the church went out and brought Miss Wide Load Wallace a special gift.
Her own titanium pew—won`t bend, won`t break.

Miss Wide Load Wallace just got back from her vacation in Paris. She was supposed to come back last week but she got stuck while walking through L'Arc de Triomphe.

56

Good & Welfare

"...makes other members feel like they're on a seesaw."

Congratulations to our own Tom Joyner who was inducted into the Radio Hall of Fame last night. All of the other inductees got together and voted that from now on it will be Tom's job to keep the hall tidy.

58

We are happy to have Brother Anderson join our Parking and Traffic Team to help direct y'all in the church parking lot. You won't have any trouble spotting him. He'll be the one with the white cane and the seeing-eye dog.

Brother Jezakiah Leech celebrated his one hundredth birthday this week--if you call nodding out at the table and drooling on your clothes celebrating.

The first annual All Blind Dart Game ended in a nothin'/nothin' tie.

59

Brother Jack Wheaton just got back from the
Annual Conference in San Francisco.
The conference was a success and he says from now on,
he wants everybody to call him "Jackeé."

TODAY'S ANNOUNCEMENTS ARE BROUGHT TO YOU BY
TYRONE'S THRIFTY MART
LOCATED IN THE HEART OF KOREATOWN.
TYRONE FIGURES THEY GOT STORES IN OUR
NEIGHBORHOOD, WHY NOT PUT ONE IN THEIRS. IT'S NOT
MAKING MONEY RIGHT NOW BUT WHAT THE HELL,
YOU KNOW WHERE HE'S LOCATED.

Holiday Notes

Kente Easter Eggs

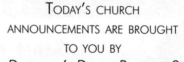

TODAY'S CHURCH
ANNOUNCEMENTS ARE BROUGHT
TO YOU BY
DRAKE DESMOND'S DRUNK REMOVAL SERVICE.
"WE GET 'EM, WE BEAT 'EM, AND WE HIDE 'EM
AWAY JUST FOR THE HOLIDAYS."

62

It's getting close to the holidays—time to suck up.
Never too old to throw in a good suck up.

On Thanksgiving Day the Missionary Board delivered four
hundred full turkey dinners to Miss Wide Load Wallace.

This announcement comes from *Mammy Made Tailor Shop.*
We'd like you to know that your Easter outfits will be ready
the Sunday after Easter.

Attention to all members and their families
who have not been to church since last Easter:
When you show up this Easter, there <u>will</u> be a cover charge.

Just a reminder to anyone who's making an Easter outfit. The
pastor would like you to know that if you have an outfit with
3 or more pieces made out of the same fabric, you will not be
allowed into church.

Another reminder, it's getting close to Easter time.
You ladies who are making your Easter hats,
if your hat is the size of a small child,
you need to pull up.

The pastor would like all kids to know if they mess up the Easter speech they will be slapped on the back of the head. How long does it take to say, "Jesus wept", huh? I mean, how do you mess that up?

65

Also we'd like to remind everybody to check out
the Christmas sale that came just in time--
Things that Kenny Stole Christmas Sale.
Remember, if you see your stuff
he'll cut you a discount.

66

Member Announcements

Sister Artell asks anyone who knows the whereabouts of her husband to tell him thanks for leaving.

Miss Wide Load Wallace had to call the paramedics over the weekend while she was taking a bath. It seems the power went out at the car wash and she got stuck between the power rinse and super dryer.

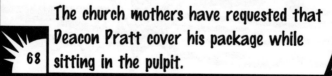

The church mothers have requested that Deacon Pratt cover his package while sitting in the pulpit.

68

TODAY'S CHURCH ANNOUNCEMENTS ARE BROUGHT TO YOU BY *KATE'S CUSS-A-GRAM*. "AT SOME POINT IN LIFE, EVERYBODY NEEDS A GOOD CUSSIN' OUT."

69

The senior choir would like to apologize to the kids who participated in the Easter egg hunt. They said they got tired and hid only six eggs. Said it seemed like more to them but it was only six.

Due to the fact that Miss Jenkins` lemonade is not moving like she thought it would, she will now sell sizes small, medium and just a swallow.

Sister Jenkins has decided to raise the price of her lemonade from 50¢ to $3.50. She says for the extra three dollars you will get a cognac bump.

It's summertime and that means it's time to get those wooden legs sanded, shellacked and rotated! So, come on down to *Wooden Leg City*, just look for the big neon wooden leg in the sky!

THE PASTOR HAS TURNED DOWN THE FOLLOWING REQUESTS:

- people who speak in tongues to do shout-outs

- spanking for sinners

- chug-a-lug communion wine night

- Miss Wide Load Wallace's suggestion for All Spandex Sunday

THE PASTOR HAS TURNED DOWN THE FOLLOWING REQUESTS:

■ Deacon Keller's request for see-through robes.

■ the youth department's request to refer to the church service as *Getting Your Prayer On*

■ the youth department's suggestion to refer to confessions as *Keeping Your Sins on the D.L.*

SPECIAL ANNOUNCMENT!

Brother Bryant got a hook-up at the phone company. So this week you won't hear "the number you have reached is not in service" when you call the prayer line.

74

The congregation has asked the women who work at the bake sale to cover their cookies and stop sitting around with their goods exposed.

TODAY'S CHURCH ANNOUNCEMENTS ARE BROUGHT TO YOU BY *POP 'EM IN THEIR MOUTH DAY CARE*. "ANYBODY CAN TEACH YOUR KIDS TO READ BUT AT *POP 'EM IN THEIR MOUTH DAY CARE*, WE KEEP THEM IN LINE."

75

The pastor would like to remind Sister Justright that he doesn't mind blessing the children but it should be done before they reach the age of 56--says its kind of hard to hold a fifty-six year old.

Sister Culpepper will join us during services next Sunday for the first time in two months--her husband has to wait until next Monday to get refills for his Viagra® prescription.

76

The next announcement comes from Wilhemina Cartwright. If you didn't get sick from her sweet potato pie that you ate last Sunday, you should have. It wasn't sweet potato.

TODAY'S CHURCH ANNOUNCEMENTS ARE BROUGHT TO YOU BY *RAY'S ANTI-BED WETTING DEVICE*. "IT'S REALLY A HEATING PAD PLUGGED INTO THE WALL, AND IT STOPS BED WETTING FOR YOUNG AND OLD."

Sister Ola Mae Mackenzie would like to know who sat behind her last Sunday. Somebody took an ink pen and played "connect the dots" with the moles on her back.

TODAY'S ANNOUNCEMENTS ARE
BROUGHT TO YOU BY
JAKE'S TWO MEAT AND
ONE GREASE RESTAURANT.
"TWO MEATS IN ONE GREASE.
EVERYBODY DOES IT,
WE'RE THE ONLY ONES WHO TELL YOU."

Here's an announcement to young Sister Weaver. Pastor says the next time your mama bends her head down to pray, please don't take your comb out to scratch the dandruff out her head. He says he doesn't care how good she says it feels, sometimes it flies all the way up here to the pulpit, and makes him feel like he's in a blizzard.

Sister Hayes would like to clear up an announcement she made in front of the church last week when she prayed for God to send her a husband.
She'd like her *own* husband--
deacons of the church need not call.

79

Due to the outburst of complaints, Reverend Packard's company, *Meat in the Mail,* has been shut down. Sounded like a good idea at the time.

All church members are asked to excuse Deacon Billard's Freudian slip last week. He meant to say Sister Sara has the best pudding in town. The best pudding. That's what he meant to say.

TODAY'S SERVICE IS BROUGHT
TO YOU BY
*TOMMY KNIGHT'S NAKED GRANDPA
BABYSITTING SERVICE.*
"WHEN YOUR GRANDPA STARTS
RUNNING AROUND NAKED AND
YOU NEED SOMEBODY TO WATCH HIM,
CALL TOMMY KNIGHT'S."

82

Still more prayers go out to Miss Wide Load Wallace. Over the weekend she choked on a whole ham and had to be rushed to the hospital--was eating hams like mints when one went down the wrong pipe.

Our prayers go out to the Reverend Seymour, the pastor of The Church on Wheels. Over the weekend the police put a boot on the church.

This sad note. Sister Murray lost her husband. He didn't pass away, she just lost him. Doesn't know where he is.

83

If you'd like to get your name on the "Something Bad Is Gonna Happen Soon" Prayer List, please see Sister Price.

What was supposed to be a very nice weekend ended in tragedy for Mrs. Warnell Pratt when she slipped in the basement and fell head first into a bundle of dirty clothes. She's in the hospital recovering from several rat bites.

84

Over the weekend Hubert Thump lost his wife of twenty-five years...to his brother.

Anyone who plans to attend Zek Tucker's funeral this afternoon, don't be surprised by the wink and grin on his face. The funeral home would like everyone to know they were pushed for time and couldn't remove them.

85

TODAY'S SERVICE IS BROUGHT
TO YOU BY
TYREE'S FETCH A HEADSTONE RENTAL:
"ONLY TIME YOU NEED A HEADSTONE IS WHEN
SOMEBODY SHOWS UP.
MIGHT AS WELL RENT."

86

Ferton Bernard passed over the weekend.
The family is asking for donations--one suit,
a pair of shoes, some teeth and a couple of dollars.

Also on this sad note. The Kings have split up after 65 years of being together. Mrs. King feels that her son needs to find his own place.

Deacon Pervis Sheets, who for so long has been in charge of the prison outreach program, is now part of the prison outreach. He got 5 to 9 for smuggling.

Our prayers go out to Miss Wide Load Wallace. Last night she had to be rushed to the Ash Institute in Buford, South Carolina.

Our get-well wishes go out to the twenty church members that took the Tae Bo® class with Miss Wide Load Wallace.

Rayford Johnson is in the hospital recovering from hip surgery. Our prayers go out to him because he went in the hospital complaining of chest pains.

88

Let us pray today not for
the sick and shut-in,
but for the people
you are sick of who
should be shut-in.

89

Six hundred pound church member Brother Lorenzo passed away over the weekend. His brother Tiny has asked that instead of flowers, donations of Ding Dongs®, Haägen-Daz®, cookies, pies, cakes and Yodels® be sent.

Tragedy struck over the weekend when Wilbert Jacobs was hospitalized for what was supposed to be a simple knee surgery. His knees were sewn on backwards and he couldn't leave the hospital.

90

Special Thank Yous

Like to thank everyone who attended the
impromptu candlelight service last night.
Wasn't supposed to be that way.
Brother Hampton didn't pay the bill.

We'd like to thank everybody who came out this weekend for the one-handed ham-bone competition.

Like to give thanks for the past weekend.
The church delivered 499 dinners.
One to the needy, 498 to Miss Wide Load Wallace.

93

Thanks go out to our senior members who made our paper
drive a success by donating the three and a half tons of
old Kleenex® out of their pockets.

The pastor would like to thank everybody who
participated in King Day last Monday.
And a reminder to Miss Wide Load Wallace:
It's King Day, not King Size Day.

94

Tithes/Offerings

The Reverend asks that instead of tithing this month, church members donate the amount equal to the weight of Miss Wide Load Wallace.

PLEASE NOTE: It's bad enough that members are taking money out of the collection plate, but taking the plate as well?

96

TODAY'S CHURCH ANNOUNCEMENTS ARE SPONSORED BY *TOMMY'S TIP FIRST RESTAURANT.* "LEAVE YOUR TIP BEFORE YOU ORDER, THEN WE'LL DECIDE WHAT KIND OF SERVICE YOU'RE GONNA GET."

97

Notice to
Brother Barass.
The pastor's sorry but you
cannot put your tithes
on layaway.

Upcoming Events

We'd like to remind everybody to go down to
the Candlelight Supper Club for
Monday Night's Shirtless Bingo.

The pastor will be calling a meeting to get the
pastor's wife to stop singing.

There will be a book signing in the lobby right
after church by Bettie Sneaks.
The book is entitled,
Nine Ways Not To See Your Grandkids.

Tickets go on sale for the gospel play
My Bad Hip's Been Giving Me Trouble.
Anyone with a bad hip will get a 10 percent discount.

THE ANNOUNCEMENTS ARE ALSO BROUGHT TO YOU BY
SKIP'S STRETCH YOUR SHOES SERVICE.
IF YOU SEE SKIP AT THE CLUB WITH YOUR SHOES ON,
HE'S JUST WORKING.
"AIN'T THAT SKIP WITH MY SHOES?"
HE'S STRETCHING THEM OUT FOR YOU, BROTHER.

101

Miss Wide Load Wallace's play,
Mama, I'm the Michelin Man,
has been cancelled. Sorry, no refunds.

You're asked to stay after church to be entertained by the
Florida State Blind Drill Team.

Mrs. Vernell's Snoot's seminar on
"The Act of Floating Bad Checks"
will be in Meeting Room 3 right after the service.

102

There are still plenty of tickets left for the play, *Mama, Why Is Wilbur Wearing Your Dress?*

If you'd like to participate in the "How Many Punches Miss Wide Load Wallace Can Take To The Throat" contest, please see Bishop Juan right after the service.

Also a reminder, next Tuesday is Christian Karaoke Night. Please see Bishop Juan after the service.

103

For tonight's evening service the pastor's topic will be "What is Hell?"
Come early and hear the senior choir practice.

104

There are still plenty of tickets for the hit play, *Mama, Mama, Mama, Mama, You 'Sleep?* Be sure to get yours.

A new event has been added this week to the church bazaar: "Guess How Many Chins Miss Wide Load Wallace Has."

TODAY'S
ANNOUNCEMENTS ARE
SPONSORED BY
SKIDER'S LEAKY EYE HOT SAUCE.
"SO HOT IT MAKES
YOUR EYES LEAK."

There are still plenty of booths left for the Sinners Expo 2000.

Usher Reminders

"Two seats over here..."

The prepaid usher program will be in effect this Sunday. If you don't pay an usher he won't help you up.

To cut down on people falling asleep in church, we're asking that members request No-Doz® toothpicks from the ushers.

TODAY'S CHURCH ANNOUNCEMENTS ARE
BROUGHT TO YOU BY
SIMMIE'S SUITS FOR SHORT MEN.
"WE HAVE A WIDE SELECTION OF BUSTER BROWN SHOES."

108

Since the
ushers have
been equipped
with stun guns,
shouting has
been cut in half.

Next Sunday the ushers will be standing by with mops, buckets and squeegees just in case Miss Wide Load Wallace starts to sweat again.

It came to our attention that Sherman Rice is this weekend's stankest usher. If you'd like to congratulate him, we're sure he'll be easy to find.

Will two of the male ushers please get a couple of ladders and a monkey wrench from the basement? We need y'all to help Miss Wide Load Wallace fasten her necklace.

110

Visiting Pastors

VISITING PASTOR

Yes, I am the Reverend C.U. Sinning, pastor of the 50% Off Church. Yes, the 50% Off Church, and it's time for the church announcements.

Please join the 50% Off Church. Whatever you've been paying to your church, we'll take half. If you've been tithing 10 percent, we'll take 5 percent.

We are asking that all baptism candidates wear protective helmets during next Sunday's baptism because the baptism pool will be half empty or half full, depending on how you look at it.

112

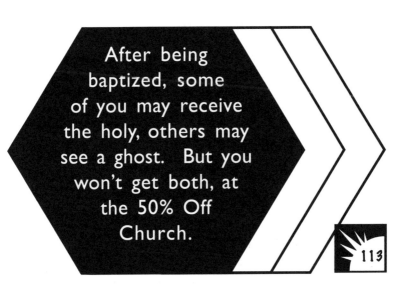

After being baptized, some of you may receive the holy, others may see a ghost. But you won't get both, at the 50% Off Church.

113

If you're sick and tired of three-hour services, at the 50% Off Church, it's only one hour and a half. We sing only half a song, preach half a sermon and if you thought your communion bread was small, come to the 50% Off Church.

At our church, you only have to give up half your sins. If you've been sleeping with the deacon's wife <u>and</u> the pastor's wife, you only have to give up the deacon's wife.

We only have five commandments. Do the best that you can with the other five.

Church Sponsors

"Sometimes you just need a big piece of meat..."

HARVEY'S
Piece of Meat

HARVEY'S BIG PIECE OF MEAT CAFÉ. Sometimes you just need a big piece of meat. A big, big, heavy, thick piece of meat. They do deliver. Just look for the trucks with the big piece of meat on top.

JACQUES' SUIT SHOP. The home of the T.D. Jacques Sweaty Suits. Anyone buying two suits will get a can of T.D. Jacques sweat.

SNAKE'S MEAT STORE. We pride ourselves in having the cleanest meat in town. Their meats may be cheaper but ours are cleaner.

BETTY'S ADD-A-MOLE SERVICE. At Betty's Add-A-Mole Service, you get one mole for $39 and a bag of moles for $150--a huge bag!

OPHELIA'S OVER-THE-SHOULDER-BOULDER-HOLDERS. Ophelia makes bras for women with really big headlights. She carries sizes Super Duper, Back Breaker and Miss Wide Load Wallace.

JANITORS WITH A LIMP JANITORIAL SERVICE. We might have a limp but we don't skip on cleaning.

Today's sponsor is the *All-You-Can-Eat-While-You're-In-Our-Restaurant*. That's right, all you can eat *in* our restaurant-- we'll be checking purses!

HUMPTY'S HOME PAYDAY LOANS. Need a little cash until payday? You don't even have to leave home. Just call Humpty up, give him your checking account or credit card number, and he'll FAX you a check in a couple of minutes.

SOAP OPERA ADDICTS ANONYMOUS. "Do you keep re-watching All My Children before you feed your children? If you burn yourself, do you watch General Hospital before going to the hospital? If so, you need to join SOAA."

ANNIE MAE'S ANTIQUES AND JUNK SHOP. Annie Mae hasn't brought any new furniture since 1957, so go on over to her house and buy some of this stuff from her. Some of it might even be worth some money.

SAMMY'S SUITS FOR SHORT MEN. Our shoe department features a large selection of Buster Browns. If you can still wear your baby shoes, Sammy's is the shop for you.

PAMELA'S PLEATHER SHOP. Get all your pleather, pleather coats and pleather pocketbooks at Pamela's. Everybody's got something made out of pleather.

BINKY'S BATHROOM VALETS. They do more than pass out towels and skeet soap. The boys from Binky's will shine your shoes while you sit in the stall. No extra cost for incense.

MILTON'S MUTT SHOP. "Don't spend hundreds of dollars on some fancy dog. Come on down to Milton's and buy a mutt. Instead of just one fancy breed, Milton's mutts have five or six in the same dog. Don't be a nut— come on down and buy a mutt."

Today's church announcements are brought to you by *Tete's Movers* where our slogan is "We can move you but hey, what the hell, something is gonna get broke. No need lying. We guarantee something is gonna get broke."

The pastor has given the congregation the go ahead to blame the first half of their lives on El Niño.

123

About the Author

J. Anthony Brown is a comedian, actor, comedy writer, radio personality, and entrepreneur. He says, "if it hadn`t been for all of those involved in this project and the grace of God-this book would have never been published. And if it had been, every last word would have been spelled wrong."

J. lives in Los Angeles with his dog.

Order Form

To order additional copies of Rev. Adenoids` Church
Announcements, please complete the order form and choose one
of the following to process your request.

Telephone orders: 877-574-4780 (toll-free)
Email orders: sales@watchoutdehnow.com
Postal orders:
KKT Publishing Company
1304 N. Highland Avenue
Suite 282
Hollywood, CA 90028
Please make checks payable to KKT Publishing Company

Order Form

NAME: _____

ADDRESS: _____

ADDRESS: _____

CITY, STATE, ZIP CODE: _____

DAYTIME PHONE NUMBER: _____

EMAIL ADDRESS: _____

_____ COPIES OF CHURCH ANNOUNCEMENTS @ $8.00 EACH _____

SHIPPING & HANDLING @ $2.95 PER BOOK _____

CA RESIDENTS ADD 8.25% TAX _____

TOTAL AMOUNT ENCLOSED _____

Order Form

To order additional copies of Rev. Adenoids` Church Announcements, please complete the order form and choose one of the following to process your request.

Telephone orders: 877-574-4780 (toll-free)
Email orders: sales@watchoutdehnow.com
Postal orders:
KKT Publishing Company
1304 N. Highland Avenue
Suite 282
Hollywood, CA 90028
Please make checks payable to KKT Publishing Company

Order Form

NAME: _____

ADDRESS: _____

ADDRESS: _____

CITY, STATE, ZIP CODE: _____

DAYTIME PHONE NUMBER: _____

EMAIL ADDRESS: _____

_____ COPIES OF CHURCH ANNOUNCEMENTS @ $8.00 EACH _____

SHIPPING & HANDLING @ $2.95 PER BOOK _____

CA RESIDENTS ADD 8.25% TAX _____

TOTAL AMOUNT ENCLOSED _____

To:

Watchoutdehnow!